Artful Memories

This edition was published in November 2021

ISBN: 978-1-7398654-0-5

To all the anonymous individuals in found photographs:
we might not know your names, but you are not forgotten.
This book is for you.

Contents

Introduction

Most of us have thousands of photographs saved on our phones that we carry with us every day. Some of us have boxes of old family photos or even older black and white snapshots of people we don't even know. Printed photographs seem to be out of fashion, yet they are very powerful objects, filled with stories and meanings. So why keep them in a box, or hidden away in the camera roll of our phones, when we can use them to create something potently unique?

Photographs are relatable objects. When we look at 'everyday' people, in their domestic environments, we discover the reality of human existence. These portraits are constant reminders of the passage of time, a memento that celebrates lives that were once lived.

Juegos de la Memoria/ Memory Play,
Silvia Pérez Sanz

Simone, Andrea Baudo Queyroulet

A photograph is always real. It's anchoring. It's a peek into someone's real past, albeit a split second of their past as the camera shutter closed. It's a lost story that presents an opportunity for rebirth.

This book is about the transformation of familiar, often mundane objects, into immortal art objects. It provides easy step by step instructions on how to transform old photographs to create a new story. But it is so much more than just an instructional book - it's a visual experience, a time travel machine, accompanied by art, quotes, inspiration galleries and even music, all personally selected by us.

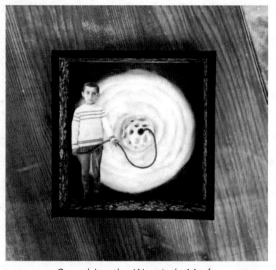

The artworks that you will find throughout the book were selected during an online open call. Artists from over 20 countries shared their personal interpretations making this book so much richer and multi-faceted.

We hope that the eclectic variety of images included will inspire you. All they have in common is that they started from a found photograph.

The way you use this book is entirely up to you and there are no boundaries to what you can explore.

Searching the Way, Lola Marín

You can use photographs of your loved ones to keep their memory alive, and to create something meaningful. You can follow a tutorial from beginning to end, or simply use it as inspiration and let the photos whisper a new story to you.

This book is not just for artists.
It's for storytellers and creatives.
It's for someone who appreciates an old, torn photograph.
It's for those who believe that lost memories can be preserved and made immortal.

Learn how to stitch on photographs, how to make memory pebbles, pocket-size keepsakes, babies napping in matchboxes, photo patchworks, woven images, and even how to alter a book to store your creations.

Welcome on board, and thank you for joining us in this quiet revolution.

NOTE: We use the term found photograph or found object to indicate something that an artist 'finds' or 'buys'. It doesn't necessarily mean found in the wild, it could come from an antique shop, an online shop, a beach, a forest, an abandoned house. It simply means that an object was chosen because of a special meaning that it holds, or an emotion that it creates. We tend to collect found objects for inspiration, or to assemble and alter to make art.

Without title, Katrin Ruhnau

Found photographs glossary

CDV or Carte de Visite is a small photograph mounted on a thin piece of card. First introduced in France in 1854 by photographer Andre Adolphe Eugene Disdéri, they became hugely popular in the latter half of the nineteenth century, and are still collected today. The typical size of a CDV is 64 by 100mm.

Cabinet Card is a photograph mounted on a piece of cardboard. It's the larger version of a Carte de Visite, and was introduced after 1870. The back contains the details of the photographers, printed or embossed with intricate designs. It usually measures 108 by 165 mm.

Magic Lantern Slide is a photograph mounted on transparent plates (usually glass). Traditionally, magic lanterns would project slides onto a wall using a light source: candles in the 17th century, lamps in the 18th and 19th century. They became popular in travelling shows, as toys and as educational tools.

RPPC or Real Photo Postcard is a photograph printed directly onto paper with a pre-printed postcard backing. They are usually black and white or sepia, but you may occasionally find some hand-coloured ones. They were introduced in 1907 by Kodak to enable people to make a postcard from any picture they took.

Jack and Jane

When we met on Instagram in March 2020, we immediately found familiarity in each other's work, and discovered that we shared a passion for old black and white photographs. We spoke a common language based on a deep love (and an almost visceral obsession) with stained papers, old photography, discarded ephemera, and the perfect imperfection of found objects.

There were countless instances when we unknowingly made very similar works at exactly the same time. Here's one of many examples: on the 21st of April 2020 we both collaged a dancer on old envelopes, stamped in green.

These images were posted on Instagram within a few minutes of each other.

Call it synchronicity (if you don't believe in magic).

Though we couldn't work together in person, we cultivated our bond across the miles, always smiling at the serendipity, every time we had the same idea about a subject, object, or colour palette, and at all times enjoying the affinity of our art and passion.

Eventually, we decided to turn this shared passion into a book, a physical space to share ideas, tips, and tricks on how to alter photographs and turn them into unique works of art.

Why photographs?

Images tell stories. When you hold a photograph in your hands, you are connecting to a person, or a place, or a moment. You look into the eyes of a stranger and find yourself. How can photographs from the past be so relevant today?

My Big Dream, Pim van Huisseling

We are all human, and more alike than we sometimes notice. We can all recognise the commonality of the human experience. We all have dreams and visions, loves and losses, victories and failures. The stories we find in old photographs are our own, because they were woven with the threads of the collective consciousness.

Bring the past into the present

When you've picked a photograph to alter, you have already created a connection between yourself and the individual in your hands. You have found the unspoken relationship between the past and the present, and you're bringing it to life by making art. And then, when you share your work, you are passing the torch so that someone else can establish their own past/present relationship, and continue this powerful journey. By connecting to your ancestors you are building a strong visual and emotional legacy.

Old photographs are a gateway to history. They carry within them an incredible amount of visual information, but they're rarely captioned, which is one of the many gifts of found photographs. The lack of captions allows for complete freedom of interpretation, and for new images and new narratives to be established.

Untitled, 10th-13th May 2017
(Stolen photograph of the sea, 24k gold leaf), Jade Gilbert

Share your story

Altering photographs makes art democratic. Each and every one of us is an artist, with our own individual stories to tell. Using photographs as a starting point creates a dialogue with the person who once, in that place and in that moment, held the camera. We don't need art skills to respond with emotions to a photograph. We are all artists.

Sometimes working with photographs can help make the unspeakable easier to speak. Anything that is difficult to express with words can become a simple visual story, and the burden of explaining is made much lighter.

By the same token, strong emotions, such as pain, or suffering, or injustice, can be hard to articulate, but they can be expressed in a visual manner by completely altering the meaning of a photograph, or even by simply giving your artwork a meaningful title.

Vestige 12, Greg Sand

Altering photographs allows any message and narrative to be presented as new. You can make visual poetry, create nostalgic images, share a political message, make art statements and push boundaries.

Be present

Altering photographs is a ritual that takes into account all that you are and all that you feel in a given moment, and turns it into art. Working with found photography allows you to be in the present moment and what you feel today looking at a photograph is never going to feel the same tomorrow.

Some days your work will be playful and ironic, on others it might be imbued with anger, or sadness, or calmness and serenity. These are all valid expressions of your state of being and what you have to contribute to the world.

Noir, Bobbie Holmes

Find healing

Working with a photograph of a loved one who has recently passed away may help to process the loss. Making an artwork that celebrates the life of that person can bring some comfort and even facilitate the grieving process. Often the simple act of going through a boxful of photographs can provide a moment of intimacy with the deceased, which can alleviate feelings of confusion and help you move towards closure and healing.

Old Love, Jennifer Black

Accept yourself

Working with photographs is an incredibly intimate, and powerful experience. By telling someone else's story you can become more aware of yourself, and you can begin to understand elements of your humanity that you hadn't quite grasped before.

Transforming an existing photograph can be less intimidating than making a start on a blank canvas, removing some fear of the blank page by giving you a starting point.

Pull the threads

Embroidery on photographs is a meditative exercise. Each stitch is a breath that connects you to a long-standing tradition of (mainly) women whose art was often dismissed as domestic craft.

With the resurgence of textile and fibre art, the age-old craft of hand-stitching is being reclaimed as an art form and it is increasingly populating gallery walls.

Pulling a thread through a photograph shows patience and resilience, qualities that aren't celebrated enough in this fast-paced, hyper-productive world.

Slowing down and focusing on a manageable task can bring calmness and reduce anxiety.

Men are Flowers, Damla Sandal

Phylogenése, Muriel Binet

Find your circle

Recontextualizing imagery requires tapping into internal beliefs and values, and can therefore help bring clarity of mind. It's also a powerful creative exercise for storytelling. When you work with found photographs, consider naming your characters, creating a context and backstory for these individuals, even if these details won't be featured in the final piece.

In the art and creative world, found photography has a growing and thriving community of artists who foster each other's creativity. You shouldn't be surprised if you receive a bunch of photographs gifted by a fellow artist, a tip about an open call, or an invitation to collaborate. Be a connector, share your knowledge, pass on the torch. It's a smaller family than you'd think.

Be daring

Found photographs are imperfect objects. They might be faded, stained, ripped, folded, oddly framed. They might be missing a corner, or have a tear on the edge. They are so imperfect, they seem just perfect to us. Imperfection calls for acceptance. Embrace the imperfection, fall in love with it, allow your own intervention to be imperfect too.

Think outside the box, go where nobody dares to go, make objects that move the viewer. The tutorials in this book can be adapted to communicate completely different meanings. Listen to the whispers, gather your memories, and make magic.

And finally, we use printed photographs because we want to preserve them, even more so now that the habit of printing photographs is rapidly vanishing. Perhaps, as a way of paying forward, we should all consider printing some more photographs, so that maybe one day, in the future, they can be found and used by other artists.

What Holds us Together, Deborah Saul

"Who are you?
What brought you to this moment when the camera went
'click' and into my hands and curious mind?
It's my hope that by creating work through combining found
photographs, book covers, paper, thread and other ephemera
that new narratives are imagined for these strangers.
They are once again treasured, thought of and loved."

Ailsa Mitchell

Using your family photographs

A lot of the projects in this book can be made personal by using family photographs.

Think about asking your relatives if they have photographs that are collecting dust and that you might be able to use, or to scan. Use this opportunity to listen. If someone in your family kept photographs for many years, they probably have many stories that have been passed on with them. Listen to those stories. Ask questions that can help you build an identity. Ask questions that can help you understand who these people are or were. By discovering facts about your ancestors you will inevitably learn something about yourself too.

Be respectful of their memory. Choose to pay homage, if that feels comfortable. Use reverence and care.

If you do find some photographs, always check on the reverse. Sometimes you will find dates, names, or helpful information that can solve attribution mysteries. If you have photographs taken in unknown locations, try doing a reverse image search on Google and see if you can identify some of the buildings. Be curious. Be a detective. This is your story too.

If you don't have access to family photographs, consider researching online. Genealogy.com, Ancestry.com, Myheritage.com, Archives.com, FamilySearch.org are a few examples of websites where you can trace your lineage and map out your ancestry. Most of these websites require subscribing. Think about gifting a family member who loves history with an annual subscription. You'll benefit too!

Beneath The Tree (Her) & Beneath The Tree (Him),
Eve Lumai Bridges

"One can't live without the past, it's always there.
The past determines our present and future
and therefore it's a gate to life."

René Alink

Where to find old photographs

Sourcing photographs is a wonderful part of the process and there are many ways for you to explore. Buying in person, if you can, is the best option. You usually find better deals, can bargain on a price, touch the paper and start creating your connection with the photos. Flea markets and antique shops are a great place for that. Sometimes you'll find boxes filled with family photographs saved by a house clearance business. Other times you will find bigger prints sold individually. Car boot, trunk, garage and yard sales are essentially different names for very similar places.

Root around in boxes, there are often hidden gems. Go early and take some cash.

Talk to house clearance companies, antique dealers, stall holders at flea markets and let them know what you're looking for; if you are a regular visitor they may put things aside for you.

An easy alternative, although nowhere near as charming, is to buy online. Ebay and Etsy are the most common places for you to browse. If you are looking for a specific subject, or topic, or location, these options will make the job a lot easier.

Finally, a newer and rising trend has blossomed from the online community of Instagram and Facebook. Explore hashtags like #foundphotos #foundphotography #antiquephotos #vernacularphotography and you might find a few gems being sold by private owners on their profile. They usually post daily and if you're quick enough to comment "me" or "sold", that photo is yours.

Being brave

Should I use an original photograph or make a copy? There is probably not a single found photograph artist out there who hasn't had this dilemma. Using original photographs can give you a connection to the people in the photograph, knowing that it captured a moment in their life, that they held the paper in their hands, showed it to their friends and family. However, there are also times when it helps to use copies.

There is no right answer and only you can decide, but here are a few things to consider:

- Is the photograph a valuable piece of your personal/family history?
- Will your family/others be upset if you use the original?
- What will happen to the photograph if you don't use it? Will it be left unseen in a box?
- Will using a copy affect the authenticity of your artwork?
- Will you treasure the artwork less if you don't use an original photograph, or will you feel regret if you do?

Remember, using an original photograph in art doesn't destroy it. It elevates it.

Sometimes making a photocopy to use in the planning stages can give you the confidence to use the original, knowing that any mistakes you might make were made on the copy.

If you decide to make a copy and want to try to replicate its aged appearance, scan the original and print it on photographic paper.

Use a fine grit sandpaper to gently scuff the edges a little.

Wrap the photograph in tissue and put it in the back pocket of your jeans for a few days so that it gets gently crumpled (the tissue prevents any dye from the jeans turning it blue).

"I am a salvage artist. My style of collage, my aesthetic, is much like a historian or archaeologist, to preserve what I unearth. I love the ancient, I swoon over beautiful penmanship and old love letters. There is a deep connection I feel to the past, to the person who penned the letter, the faces in a photograph, the beauty and the decay. Bits of ephemera, some centuries apart, are combined through folding, tearing, layering and peeling back, exposing an identity lost and creating a new history. The Japanese word, Mottainai, meaning 'too good to waste,' was used to describe boro fabric: textiles that have been mended and patched over and over. This resonates with me, so every scrap of antique paper or vintage fabric is saved until it finds a home in my art. I also feel the importance of using the original materials, not copies, to lend authenticity to myself and the voice I'm hoping to bring to the original owner of the document or photograph. 'Human flourishing is the epic marker on your work, investing in the ups and downs.' Royal Alley-Barnes, CoCA."

Colleen Monette

Adams Schwestern, Anna Müller

Erased, Colleen Monette

The Joy, Ian Tothill

Making art that works

It's not always easy to pinpoint what it is about a piece of art that makes it work. It can often be subtle touches that transform a piece. The projects in this book will invite you to combine photographs with other media and materials, so knowing a little about design theory will help you. There are numerous books that can guide you in detail on the principles and elements of design should you wish to explore. We've picked out some very basic design pointers that will help you to create pieces that you love as you work through the projects in this book.

Contrasts

Contrasts make artwork more interesting. Think about adding contrasts:
- dark and light shades
- smooth and rough textures
- organic and geometric shapes

Rule of thirds

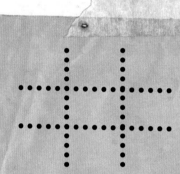

Imagine your page has been split with two horizontal and two vertical lines.

Placing the subject of your composition along one of those lines, or where they intersect, can make it much more appealing than placing the focal point in the centre.

Colour palette

Consider how many colours you want to use and whether they will be similar e.g. blue and green, or contrasting e.g. red and green.

Using similar colours, or shades of the same colour, will be more harmonious. Using contrasting colours will be more vibrant. Consider which will work best with the subject matter of your photographs.

Rule of odds

Aim for an odd number of focal points e.g. three rather than two. An odd number helps your eye travel around a piece of art and makes it feel more balanced.

Working with

paint

Absence, Francesca Artoni

Adding media to photographs

Adding paint, pen, pencil or crayon is a simple and very effective way of altering photographs. The shiny surface of photographs will accept some media such as acrylic paint, Posca markers or marker pens, but not others such as ink and pencil, so you may need to prepare the surface first with gesso. Gesso is a primer and is available in black, white and clear. It provides some 'tooth' to the surface to enable other products to then be added.

In this example, the photograph had a very glossy surface. A coat of black gesso was applied to the background and left to dry.

Once the gesso had dried a circle was drawn with pencil for the outline of the moon and filled with acrylic paint. The stars were applied with a white Uni-Ball Signo pen.

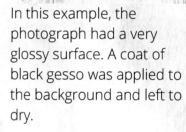

Clear gesso was painted over the figures, which produced a fine gritty surface enabling coloured pencil to be added. Take care if using a wet media over the clear gesso as it might 'wash' the gesso off if the initial surface was very glossy.

Gentlewoman 009, Naomi Vona

Springtime Roses, Twiggy Boyer

Using felt tips

An alternative to gesso and paints are felt tip (marker) pens. The main difference here is that, instead of blocking out details of the photo by using thick colours, you are playing with transparencies letting some elements of the photograph still show. This technique works particularly well with lighter colours but due to the reflective nature of the photographic paper, it might require more than one coat. See in this example how the shadows on the shorts created by the folds are still visible once the colour has dried, and in fact, all those details are now enhanced by the colour.

In the following example we used fineliners, which allowed for more detailed work. Since photographic paper is not porous the colour does not sink in but instead sits on top of the photograph coating. Here are a few tips to help you navigate this difference.

When you lift the pen off the photograph, it might leave a dot of wet ink. Try and limit these by:

- working in large sections without lifting the pen
- using a soft tissue to quickly wipe these dots off the paper
- dragging your wet dot to a corner or a darker section of the photograph

Please note: this technique only works on photographs with a glossy finish. Using fineliners on older, matte photographs may scratch the surface and therefore damage the image.

Rose and Harold, Kelly Bymers

Lizzie & Walter, Janet Reid

Pathways, Sonya Carnes

Rapture of the Deep, Debbie Keller

Isolating an image

Isolating part of an image is a great technique for changing the context of a photograph. In the same way that digital artists might remove a background using photo editing software, you can obscure a photograph's background by using pens or paint, giving you beautiful textures and imperfections that you don't get with digital art.

This photograph had lots of energy but much of it was lost in the dark background. By painting the background with this mint green colour, the photograph was brought to life and elements such as the bicycle became more visible.

 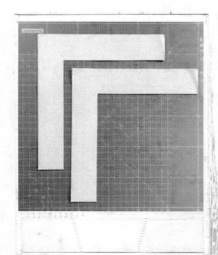 

To start, use a small paint brush or a pen to draw around the outline of the section that you want to isolate. Once you have a clean outline, you can fill in the rest of the background.

Think about how you could crop your photograph to improve the composition. Use two L-shaped pieces of card (you can cut these from an old picture mount). Place them on top of the photograph and try different ways of cropping the image.

Heather's Birthday, Kamryn Shawron

Fishing from home. FFH.
Lucía D'Elía Lago

Domandami, Valentina Cozzi

Yes to the Dress, Ottavia Marchiori

Working with *containers*

Just the act of enclosing something in a container makes it feel precious. There's that magical moment of anticipation as you open it to reveal what's inside. Tins and containers give you a ready-made stage for your photographic art. They act as a frame and allow you to add 3D elements.

The options for making art in containers are endless. Keep your eyes open for tins, boxes, and pots, the more weird and wonderful, the better!

Contemplation, Studio Four Corners

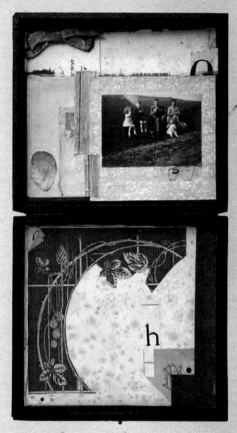

On the Way Home, Zoë Heath

Rockfall, Mano Kellner

"Every photograph is like a time capsule, a moment that was somehow important enough for someone to want to capture it and give it a place in the future. Working with old photographs feels like digging up the time capsules that were somehow forgotten - and trying to give them meaning again, before sending them off to another future."
Cindy Kuijpers

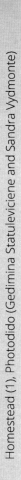

Homestead (1), Photodido (Gedimina Statuleviciene and Sandra Vydmonte)

A Treasury of Dissolution, no.9, Anna van der Putte

"There is something both intriguing and comforting in the timeless aspect of the human experience. Photos from so long ago can be so easy to relate to, and creating with them feels like a tribute to the fact that indeed we are so much the same over all the years of time."

Ramona Samuels

The traveller

Project

You will need:

- Rectangular tin with a lid (ours was 6x9.5cm).
- Brown parcel paper
- Tracing paper
- Patterned paper for the lining
- Brown acrylic paint
- Sticky foam pads
- Photograph
- Glue (Mod Podge or PVA)
- Craft knife or scalpel
- Old letter, envelope or postcard

To convert cm to inches see page 148

There's something very charming about opening this tiny suitcase to find the little girl stepping out into the world. It would make a lovely gift; maybe for a loved one setting off on travels or honeymoon. See the wedding version in the Explore section.

Choosing a photograph

The main requirement is that the subject looks as though they are ready to travel. Choose an image with visual clues such as an overcoat and some sort of bag. If you don't have a suitable photograph you could scan the one at the end of the book and resize accordingly to print.

The photograph should fit inside your tin with roughly 1cm space around the edges as shown.

Choosing the lining paper

Most old suitcases were lined with a patterned paper. You could choose any pattern you like for yours but think about the scale. You may need to reduce the size of the print so that it looks proportionate to the size of the tin/suitcase.

This project could be adapted for any time period by changing the papers that you use.

1

If your photograph is on lightweight paper, glue it to a piece of card to strengthen it. Cut out the photograph.

29

2

Make templates for the inside of the tin by placing your tracing paper into the lid and then running your fingernail around the edge to mark it. Cut it out. Repeat for the main part of the tin so that you have a template for each.

3

Use the template to cut a piece of your patterned lining paper for the lid.

4

Glue the lining paper into the lid.

.

5

Measure the depth of the sides of the tin and the lid. Cut strips of lining paper to the same depth.

6

Glue the strips to the sides of the interior of the tin and lid and press firmly in place.

7

Use the tracing paper template to choose which part of your envelope (or chosen paper) you want to use as the background. Cut around the template.

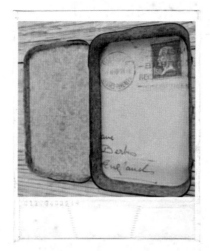

8

Glue the envelope piece into the tin.

9

Attach foam pads to the back of the photograph, ensuring that they can't be seen from the front. We used two stacked on top of each other to make the photograph stand out from the background.

10

Carefully place the photograph centrally in the tin and press to adhere.

11

Draw around the outline of the tin onto the brown parcel paper. Add a border all around so that it is large enough to cover the sides of the tin.

12

Trim the edges so that they are the same height as the sides of the tin. Snip the edges of the paper on each corner.

13

Glue the paper to the tin and press the snipped corners down to work around the curves.

14

Repeat this for the lid so that the outside of the lid and tin are both covered.

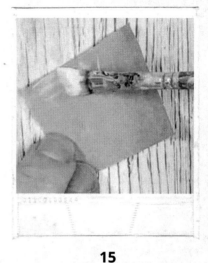

15

Make the suitcase handle by cutting a piece of brown paper and adding glue to one edge. Ours was about 5x3.8cm. Adjust yours to the size of your tin.

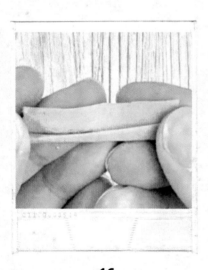

16

Roll the paper from the dry end to the glued end to make a tight roll.

17

Place the rolled paper onto the side of the tin and glue the ends down with a strip of brown paper so that it stands proud of the tin, forming a handle shape.

18

Use brown acrylic paint to coat a small piece of paper. You will need enough to cut four small circles - see next photograph.

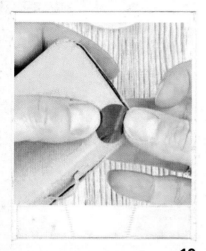

19

Press a circle onto each corner of the main part of the tin.

20

Add additional elements as desired such as dried leaves to the bottom of the tin.

Explore!

There are so many ways to develop this idea. Try:

- different sizes and shapes of tins
- using fabric to line the tin
- different colour palettes
- including personal objects that belonged to the person in your photograph

Somewhere in Time, Sarah Perkins

Siren, Beverly Silva

Dancing Queen, Mauricio Mo

The Future is FEMALE!, Anke Teuscher

Dasein Sosein Sein, Silke Kreuznacht

Simple 3D Scene

1-hour project

The simple act of cutting out the focal point of a photograph and letting it stand proud against a different background can give the image new life. Combining it with other documents, backgrounds or images creates a new narrative.

In this variation of the previous project, the photograph was paired with a piece of a vintage map and an old postcard which draws one in to imagine the travels of these three women.

You will need:

- Shallow box or lid (ours was 1.3cm deep)
- Photograph that fits easily within the box
- Old papers
- Sticky foam pads
- PVA glue or Mod Podge
- Piece of cardboard
- Scissors
- Craft knife or scalpel

1

Choose some papers that will help tell your story. We used a piece of a map and the handwritten side of an old postcard.

2

Coat your box with glued paper (or your map if you're using one), leaving the inside face uncovered.

3

Cut your letter/postcard to the size of the inside of your box and glue in place.

4

Cut out the main image from your photograph accurately, leaving a strip along the bottom so the figures don't appear to be floating in space.

5

Attach a piece of card and some sticky foam pads to the back of the photograph to create depth. Make sure the card cannot be seen from the front.

6

Peel the backing paper from the sticky foam pads and attach the photograph to the background.

Explore!

Think of ways to create 3D scenes. For the diver (left), we used layers of cardboard, the dog piece (below) had a frame inset and the ski lift piece (right) had wires acting as supports for the photographs.

"I am drawn to found photographs because they expose the temporality of life. 'By giving me the absolute past of the pose... the photograph tells me death in the future... I shudder over a catastrophe which has already occurred.' These words from Roland Barthes' Camera Lucida precisely describe how I feel when I consider a photograph so old that the subject must be dead. My response has a number of layers: I feel an immediate connection to the living person in the photograph, followed by a dread of what inevitably is to come for them, completed by a sense of grief over what has, of course, already transpired."

Greg Sand

Light My Fire 2, Pat Laffin

Sleeping in a matchbox

Project

LUCKY-FOUR

PIONEER MATCHES

FRONTLINE

THE LION MATCH Co. Ltd.

The PILOT MATCH

♫ Dustin O'Halloran - Opus 36

You will need:

- Small photo of a sleeping baby (or adult)
- Vintage matchbox
- Cotton wool
- Tea bag
- 2mm glass beads
- Cotton thread
- Needle
- Craft knife or scissors
- Cutting mat
- PVA glue or Mod Podge
- Paper

A smaller alternative to tins are old matchboxes, which are perfect for this project. They can be filled with any little found treasures and can become precious keepsakes, so let your imagination go wild.

1

Make yourself a cup of tea and keep the teabag. Add water to a small bowl and dip the tea bag to make a very weak, pale-coloured tea. Use this mixture to lightly stain a handful of cotton wool. Put aside to dry.

2

Find a photograph of a baby or adult, asleep or laying down. If the photo is too big or too small for the matchbox, scale it up or down with a printer or photocopier. It needs to fit snugly inside your matchbox.

3

Cut out the photograph using scissors or a craft knife. (If you're using a print, instead of an original, you may need to reinforce it by glueing it on a thicker piece of paper or interfacing). See page 94

4

Thread a needle and secure the end with a knot. Bring the needle up from the back of the photograph, insert a bead or two, and then take it down through the front, a short distance away. Repeat this process to cover the whole dress with beads. At the end, tie another knot.

5

Once your stained cotton is fully dry, insert it inside the matchbox.

6

The photograph can be glued in place with a dab of PVA glue or left loose, the choice is yours.

This tutorial is a fun and creative way to 'frame' old photographs of your sleeping children...

Explore!

...and it works well with grown-ups too!

Treasures inside jewellery boxes

"We were the children who picked up leaves and stones and treasured them like diamonds.
We were the children who filled up bottles of sand from every beach.
We were the children who collected feathers and branches and stories in their pockets.
We were the children who made jewellery out of daisies and books out of dreams.

We are the archaeologists of beauty, who salvage the lost and discarded to return it to life.
We are the collectors of the rusty and the odd.
We are the storytellers of the forgotten.
We sing of crippled dancers and unrequited loves, of loneliness, of lust, freaks, and clowns.
We still make books out of dreams and carry stories inside our pockets."
JR

Were you the kind of child who would pick up pebbles and feathers to take home? If you were, you probably still are, or you should pay a visit to your inner child. And if you think, just like we do, that found photographs are precious things, then the idea of placing them inside jewellery boxes shouldn't seem too strange. This won't be a step by step tutorial, more an invitation to play.

Gather your little treasures and a photograph, and create a little box of precious finds.

Replace rings and earrings with tiny found objects that create a connection with the photograph. Think buttons, little rusty objects, shells, dried flowers. There are no rules except what you deem valuable.

Just like jewellery, these are great to keep, but even better to give.

An alternative to jewellery boxes are old rusty tins, which already come filled with charm and stories. Think of them as little homes. You can place a photograph of a house that was meaningful to you, or your family, on the lid. And you can fill the tin with little memories from that place. Keys, dried flowers from the garden, fragments of wood from the fence, anything that takes you back to a place, even if you didn't know it.

Anemoia is a word coined by
The Dictionary of Obscure Sorrows,
which means: nostalgia for a time
you've never known.

Consider creating a time capsule within a tin, seal it and open it in ten years' time.

It will take your breath away.

43

"A full-colour image tells a complete story.

A black and white photo tells half a story.

We write the rest."

JR

Working with

paper

Altering a background with collage

A great alternative to painting is collage. By removing the original background and replacing it with paper, you can completely alter the meaning of the photo. In this example, a series of vintage paper strips are arranged to create a rainbow behind the two figures. The original white border of the photograph was kept to frame the new work.

You can also paste items on top of a photograph to tell a new story. It's easy to create striking images using modern elements on top of a vintage photograph, like the telephone, light fixture and 70s wallpaper in this Carte de Visite. Impossible and anachronistic pairings are quintessentially collage.

Brave choices and contrasting elements often make for iconic images.

Combining personal documents with photographs can produce powerful pairings.

This photograph of an airman has paper with his own handwriting inserted as the background, creating a greater connection to the photograph.

Here the background was cut out and replaced by a poem written by the sweetheart of the woman in the photograph.

Photograph cubes

This is a simple but very effective way of combining photographs and ephemera. Think about the papers that you select; maybe use pieces that belonged to the people in the photographs, pieces of their handwriting, wallpaper, documents, book pages. Use a variety of shades for added interest.

You will need:
- Photographs
- Old papers
- Wooden cubes
- Glue (Mod Podge or PVA)
- Scissors or scalpel

Decide whether you will use one image or piece of paper per side, or collage several smaller pieces.

Cut or tear pieces of your photographs and papers and glue them to the sides of your cubes.

Use your scissors or scalpel to trim any bits that stick out over the edges.

Blocked Memories, Elizabeth Burman

"Found photographs provoke unanswerable questions. These strangers represent faded memories, an anonymous snapshot into another reality. Undefined and malleable, their past unknown, they enable new narratives to be woven. These images have become an inexplicit memorial, conveying a sense of fragmentation and loss."

Frances Willoughby

Dreamer, Xoana Elias

"Black and white photography erases time from the equation."

Jason Peterson

Casulo III (Cocoon III), Cláudia Brandão

All dressed up

Project

♫ Doris Day - More

50

You will need:

- Paper - about the weight of copier paper (80gsm). We used old blank pages from a text book. If you are using patterned paper, copy the pattern to both sides.
- Photograph of a person, cut out. If your photograph is quite flexible, attach it to some card first.
- Scissors and a round object or compasses, or a circle cutter
- Glue - we used Mod Podge
- Ruler

To convert cm to inches see page 148

This is a beautiful way to bring a photograph to life. Cutting the figure out from the background and allowing it so stand upright helps you to relate to the person more, to see them as more than a 2D image on a piece of old paper.

This project is adapted from a design for a tiny book by Kit Davey. Kit makes delightful, unusual artworks from found materials. To see her work and online classes go to www.found-object-art.com.

1

Work out what size of circles you need by measuring your photograph from the figure's waist to the top of the head (crown). This measurement will be the radius of your circles. Set your compasses or circle cutter to this measurement. The waist to crown measurement of our photograph is 4cm.

If you don't have compasses or a circle cutter find a round object that has a diameter of twice your waist to top of head measurement so, in our case, something that is 8cm across.

Draw and cut out 10 circles.

Quick reminder!

Radius is the measurement from the centre of a circle to the edge

Diameter is the measurement from edge to edge through the centre of a circle

2
Fold a circle in half.

3
Fold the circle in half again so that you have a quarter circle.

4
Unfold the circle.

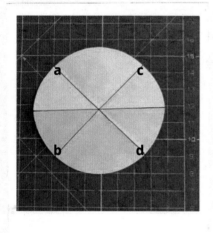

5
Fold the circle in half again half way between two of the existing folds so that point 'a' touches point 'b' and point 'c' touches point 'd'.
The folds should then look as shown.

6
Push the new fold line backwards so that the circle sides fold in and you can press it flat as shown.

When folded flat it should look like a quarter circle.

Repeat these steps for each circle.

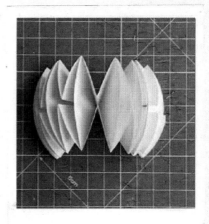

7

Apply some glue to cover one of the flat sides.

8

Press the glued side to a flat side of another piece to join the two together as shown.

9

Continue until all of the pieces are glued together.

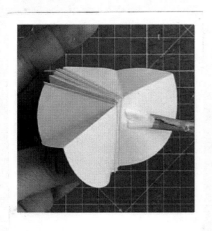

10

When you have joined all the pieces together apply some glue to one end and attach it to the other end to create a circular shape which will be the base for your 'doll'.

When you place the base on a flat surface it will stand up as shown. If necessary, press the top lightly so that all the folded points meet at the top centre.

11

Place your photograph next to your base so that the person's waist is level with the top of the base. If the photograph is too high, cut the bottom of the photograph off just above the bottom of the base.

12

Make a slit from the bottom of your photograph up to the centre of the waist as shown. The slit needs to be slightly wider at the bottom than the top. The slit in the example is 2mm wide at the bottom.

13

Slide the photograph down onto the base. The split in the photograph will act like a clip, holding the two sides of the base together.

Half-height fold

If your photograph won't slide down to the bottom of the base it could be because:

- your photograph is taller than the base, in which case, trim a small amount off the bottom of the photograph

- you have pushed the photograph into one of the half-height folds. Take it out and ensure that you are pushing it down either side of a half-height fold (see illustration).

14

Adjust the position of the photograph on the base until you are happy with it. We usually have more of the folds in front of the figure than behind so that the skirt looks very full from the front. Add a dab of glue to hold the front of the skirt to the figure if needed.

Explore!

This folding technique can be adapted in many ways.

How about using a photograph from a first communion or a ballet performance? Using a lace doily would create a great lacy skirt. Or a school prom? If you have some similar fabric you could photocopy that to use for your circles so that they match the photograph.

Antique sepia photographs

These are antique cabinet card photographs.

Right - We used sepia illustrations from an old book for the circles. If you don't have any, you can make some by scanning an illustrated book page and using basic editing software to change the colour to sepia before printing.

Left - We printed some tartan (plaid) in sepia colours on both sides of the paper for the kilt to match the Scotsman photograph.

Double-sided Frame

This technique is perfect for making keepsakes or gifts. We combined a wedding photograph with silk and lace from a wedding dress and a baby photograph with dried flowers to create a meaningful memento. The metal and glass hinged frame was inexpensive and bought online.

1-hour project

You will need:

- Small double-sided glass hanging frame
- Photographs
- Piece of cardboard
- PVA glue or Mod Podge
- Craft knife or scalpel
- Decoration such as fabric scraps, dried flowers

1

2

3

4

1
Cut your photographs to the same size as the inner edge of the frame

2
Accurately cut out the subjects of the photographs.

3
Cut your card to the size of the inside of the frame.

4
Collage the photographs and decorative elements to both sides of the card.

'To Carmen and Abel, With Love´, Cindy Kuijpers

"I've always had a penchant for collecting historical curio and forsaken ephemera, especially found objects such as old photographs that have the 'perfectly imperfect' evidence of being time-worn. These photos, along with other gathered artwork ingredients, are given a second chance at life, playing the roles of supporting cast members in my world of mixed-media choreographies."

Karla Fuller

Dearest, Maggie Horvath

Family Tree, Denise ((bonaimo)) Sarram

"Leafing through old photo albums, faded memories slip off the pages; the crumbled, cracked glue no longer keeps yours and those of strangers locked in place. No certainty of who the people are, where the photos were taken. The truth is like a parchment sheet covering the black-and-white photographs. Milky and blurry, there is room for individual interpretation. I entered this space by collecting strangers' photographs at flea markets to reinvent the stories behind these photographs, to rewrite their histories, because the people that once remembered were long gone. Each photo is unique and yet strangely familiar; the kind of photo one might have stumbled across in the attic or basement of a relative's house. Memory does not rely on truth or facts. Our own personal memories are constantly re-shaped and re-imagined, always in flux, but always attached to certain motifs and the somewhat fanciful, magical. I tried to capture these motifs and harmonies in my work, whether true or false."

Claudia Grabowski

The Star Tsar, Nichola Bendall

Une Petite Fille ~ Granddaughter, Karla Fuller

Working with

books

Magic lantern book

♫ A.R. Rahman - Yeh Jo Des Hai Tera

You will need:

- Magic lantern slide
- Battery sensor light
- Old book (must be thicker than the sensor light)
- 50cm ribbon
- Craft knife or scalpel
- Pencil
- Cutting mat
- PVA glue
- Hot glue

Magic lantern slides are precious collector's objects, but they can be hard to display. In this tutorial you'll learn how to make your slide the main character of its story by housing it inside an illuminated book.

Consider playing with transparencies by layering images on translucent sheets, or adding coloured tissue paper, or even stack multiple slides.

1
With a pencil draw the outline of the slide in the centre of the book cover.

2
Insert a cutting mat between the book cover and the pages and, using a sharp craft knife, cut inside the lines. Remove the square.

3

Leave the first book page blank. This will serve as a filter between the light and the slide. In the centre of the second page mark the outline of the light and draw a square leaving at least 2cm extra all around.

4

Working with no more than 15 pages at a time cut out the squares with a craft knife. Continue carving the book, regularly checking that the sensor light fits inside the hole when the book is closed. If the hole becomes too narrow, adjust the square size accordingly.

5

Once you've cut out all the pages, brush the borders of the book, both on the inside and outside, with PVA glue. To avoid glueing the pages to the covers use sheets of wax paper to isolate. Repeat this process a second time once the glue has fully dried.

6

Place your slide inside the cover and apply a line of hot glue all around the edge to keep in place inside the cover. Let dry.

7

Cut out 2 paper circles slightly wider than your ribbon, and trim about 1/3 off. Cut the ribbon in half.

8

Measure the height of the book cover and mark the halfway point. Glue the ribbons in place and then cover with your paper circles.

9

Brush PVA glue onto the inside of the book cover, avoiding the slide. Close the book so that it sticks to the blank page. When dry, open the book and glue the blank page to the rest of the book to create a filter.

10

In the picture above you can see the filter page under the cutout square.
Align the sensor light with the cutout square and glue in place on the back cover.

11

To finish everything off, you may want to cover the spine with your own title.

Notes

We use sensor lights that only activate for 20/30 seconds to avoid damaging vintage slides with direct light. For longer illumination time, you can use fairy lights or LED strips instead. Sensor lights can be found in homeware stores as cupboard and wardrobe wireless lighting.

Magic lantern slides can sometimes be found in antique stores, and easily purchased online. If sourcing glass slides is difficult, this tutorial can be easily adapted with the use of plastic 35mm slides that you may already have. An alternative is to print your images on acetate sheets and use them instead of slides.

Tips for book carving

- Use a sharp new blade.

- Once you've figured out what size your hole needs to be, cut out a square of the same size from a board and use it as a guide.

- Place a cutting mat under the pages you're cutting to avoid little strips shredding around the border.

- Cut out the last page individually, making sure it's a neat square, as this is the only page that will be fully visible once you've glued the pages together.

- If the edges look a bit rough, you may sand them with sandpaper before glueing.

- Little tears and rips might happen, but most won't be visible once you've glued the pages together. They make for a more handmade look, when you hand-cut without a machine. Embrace the imperfection.

"Working with old photographs allows us to give a second chance to lost memories."

Ottavia Marchiori

Losing my Mind, Natasha Pastrana

these islands of sanctuary

in an ocean of

loneliness

Ocean of Loneliness, Carrie Mason

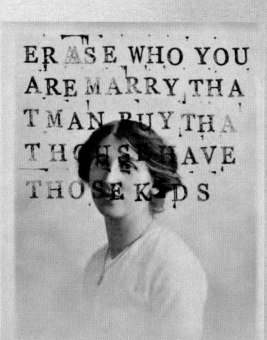

ERASE WHO YOU
ARE MARRY THA
T MAN BUY THA
T HOUSE HAVE
THOSE KIDS

Erase Who You Are, Lana Turner

Jane Eyre Steam Punked, Wilma Millette

Art journaling

Keeping an art journal is a creative way to explore your thoughts and feelings. An art journal is a place to play, and to try different techniques and materials without feeling that you have to make a work of art. There are no rules, and you can use any medium you like; collage, paint, stencils, words, and, of course, old photographs. It can be a powerful tool for self-expression.

You can use found photographs as a way to illustrate a sentiment, tell a story, or to represent yourself.

Last of the Snowdrops, Sofia Shearring

Art journals, or artist journals, are a daily creative practice of self-care. An art journal can be used to explore new techniques without worrying about the outcome, or to try new media and colour combinations. It can also be used as a visual diary that keeps a record of events and emotions. It can even be used as a healing medium to process feelings and to de-stress.

There are no rules as to what can and can't be put in a journal. Some artists will only have visual explorations. Others might include handwriting, quotes, or process notes to document ideas.

I am a Universe, Susie Lafond

Above - "This is a page from one of my art journals, made on the day that my mum passed away. I don't tend to write about my thoughts or feelings so this was an important way for me to start processing my emotions, without any concern about the artistic merit of what I was making." JC

You can use any journal for this purpose. A blank sketchbook can be a great start, and it can be painted, collaged, ripped and stitched. It's a sacred space for you to navigate through learning and play, and it's uniquely yours. A fun and greatly satisfying alternative to a sketchbook is to make your own book following a simple bookbinding tutorial.

If blank pages seem too daunting for you, consider using an old book as a medium to be turned into a scrapbook. See pages 71-73 for a few tips on altering pre-existing books.

Beach Day, Victoria Gray

Character, Claire Steele

"A photograph is a fleeting moment, made still. It arrives alone into the present with its own emotional luminosity. There is no way of knowing whether the story it tells was true, it offers itself as a kind of half-life, almost on the point of vanishing. I love symbolic language, the way meaning layers itself, offers up different readings, in different lights, but that these are suggestive and might never rise to the surface. Even so, the surface is itself a pleasing place to rest the eye.

The image I made with this photo, was made as a page in a book as a gift for a friend who was dying. It would be the last birthday present. The word character means letters, notes, marks on the page, person in a fiction and personality. The word comes from the Greek for engraving, clear and distinctive marks signifying ownership. The image I made also speaks of the music of love, how clear that is in relation to the indistinct photograph of a man and a child in a garden. It suggests the way relationships fade and blur but the fragrance that is particular to one moment might perfume our whole lives. The B flat Major Sixth chord was held by Schubert to be 'a quaint creature.' All of these things were part of the gift of this page of the book. I like working with old photographs, rescuing them from the past and imbuing them with new stories. They reveal to us what was once valued enough to be preserved, and adapting them, embellishing them with new narrative energy, offers an opportunity to re-imagine the kind of beauty that makes life worth living."

Claire Steele

Full of Quiet, Lisa Goddard

Time To Rebuild, Ramona Samuels

69

Brave Girl, Nicole Watson

Layers of Life - Victorian Photo Album, Sabine Remy

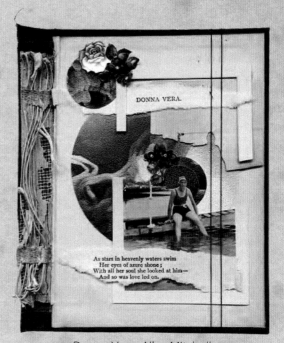

Donna Vera, Ailsa Mitchell

Stanford, Margarete Miller

Altered books

An alternative to working in a sketchbook or handmade journal is to repurpose an old book. An altered book can be a great option for collating you artworks. It allows your art to be portable and tactile, as well as allowing your pieces to tell a story in a familiar format.

Most of us were taught to protect our books and keep them in good condition, so cutting, painting, and collaging on them might feel uncomfortable. However, just a glance at the number of unwanted books in charity shops should help to ease your conscience. Many of the books that we use in artworks haven't been looked at for many years. When they are transformed into art they become a thing of value once again, albeit for a different reason.

Choosing a book - the type of book you choose will depend on how you intend to use it. Ours include small softback books such as an antique hymnal (about postcard size) used for simple collages, large hardback books and a range in-between. If you plan to have a theme to your artwork, then a book about a relevant topic may work well, particularly if you plan to keep the cover or some pages as they are.

This old bird textbook was the perfect choice for collages using old photographs and bird images which were added onto the pages that had no illustrations.

Size - this will depend on how large you like to work. If you are using original old photographs, think about what size they are and what else you will add to the pages so you have the right amount of space.

Hardback or paperback - hardback books are usually the best option as the cover will protect your artwork better. They also tend to have stronger bindings which means that the book is less likely to fall apart if you start removing or adding pages.

Type of paper - the main consideration is the strength of the paper. Some old books become very fragile and the pages won't stand up to the addition of any media. Fold some of the pages. If they are brittle and break when folded they won't be suitable for this project. Some old books have paper with a high clay content which have a very smooth, almost silky finish; others are very woody and fibrous and it's a case of personal preference as to which you choose.

Preparing an altered book

You will need:

- Old book
- Acid free book-binding tape or, if your book doesn't need to be archival, use any tape such as masking or medical (micropore) tape
- Glue
- White gesso

Prior to using an old book, it may need strengthening and a few of the pages removing to make space for the photographs and other media you plan to add to the pages.

The instructions below are for creating a 'blank canvas' from a book but you could choose to use less gesso and keep some of the text and images.

1

Check if the book is securely attached to the cover. If necessary, secure it using tape.

2

Carefully remove about a quarter of the pages

3

If the pages are made of thin paper, glue them together in pairs to make them stronger.

4

Apply a coat of gesso to each page to cover the text and make a blank base.

5

Check that all of the pages are securely attached and apply tape to the join if required.

6

Your book is now ready to be used.

"The examples above all come from the same altered book. I wanted this book to celebrate all forms of love, so I chose a book of love poems by Christina Rossetti, as a starting point. The substrate (base) was altered with found photographs, vintage papers, gold leaf, rusty staples, ink, thread, lace and pressed flowers. The book is about love, loss and healing, and the poems were used to inform some of the stories of human connection, marital love, affection between siblings, same-sex love, friendship and love and worship of nature." JR

Left - This book was made by altering a small children's board book. It measures 85mm and has 12 pages. Because of the thickness of the pages, board books are ideal to alter with collage as the glue won't warp the board. They also open flat, so you can easily work across both pages. This book is titled "A Few Satisfactory Experiments" as it was used to try techniques and colour combinations, so it is effectively a small art journal, derived from a pre-existing book.

"The pages below are from an altered book that I made in the early days of the Covid 19 pandemic. In response to the constant, horrific news and my observation of how thin the veneer of civilisation is when society is faced with a serious threat, I needed to create a calm place. The base was an old hardback novel. I used vintage papers, photographs, silk, stitch, dried flowers, ink, leaf monoprints, paint and encaustic wax." JC

Hail Mary, Emily Glink

Child, Larysa Hnativ

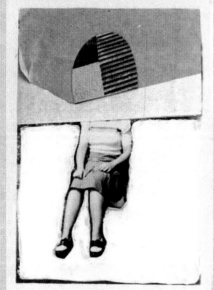

Sitting Meditation /Headspace Series,
Agnieszka Zając

Image transfers

You will need:

- Laser copy of a photograph
- Matte medium such as Mod Podge
- Substrate (base) - ours was a collaged page
- Microglaze or cooking oil

It's important to use a laser printer for your photocopy. With a laser print, the image sits on the surface of the paper and can be lifted off with the matte medium, whilst an inkjet print is absorbed into the paper and will not transfer as well.

An alternative to using an original photograph in your artwork is to make an image transfer, particularly if you want the substrate, in this case some typed and handwritten text, to show through, as the transfer will be slightly transparent.

There are several techniques that can be used to transfer printed images. This one is done using matte medium. The image will be mirrored when transferred; this matters most if you're using text as it will be back to front, so reverse it before you print.

1
Cut out your photocopied image and paint over the whole image with matte medium.

2
Place the image face down and smooth it onto your background. Leave until very dry.

3
Apply clean water to the back of the image and rub gently to remove the white paper.

4
Keep adding water and rubbing gently until the white paper has rubbed away.

5
Leave to dry. Rub a little Microglaze or cooking oil into the picture to make it clearer if required.

Echoes II, Jo Hudson

By The Sea, Emily Glink

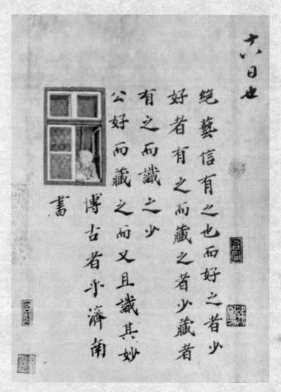

Writings on the Wall, Steven Jans

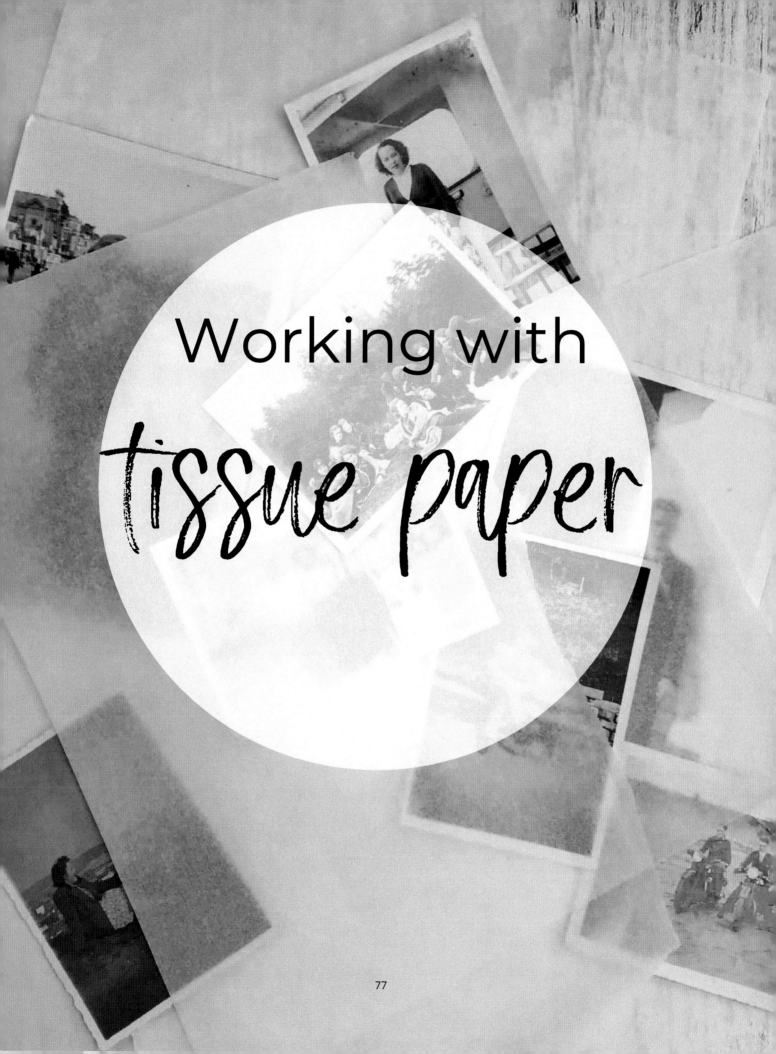

Working with
tissue paper

Printing on tissue paper

You will need:

- Digital scan of a photograph
- Scissors
- Printer
- Tissue paper - the most transparent that you can find, and acid-free
- Spray mount - repositionable
- Piece of printer paper to use as a carrier sheet

Learning to print onto tissue paper opens up some wonderful artistic techniques. Tissue prints enable you to collage onto delicate surfaces and to create layers of images and text.

This is our preferred technique, but some artists attach the tissue to the printer paper with a glue stick by applying glue around the margin of the paper instead of using spray mount. See which technique works best with your printer.

1

Cut your tissue paper to slightly larger than a sheet of printer paper.

2

Spray your printer paper with repositionable spray mount.

3

Lay your tissue paper onto the printer paper and smooth to remove any wrinkles. Trim the edges to the same size as the printer paper.

4

Feed the paper into your printer ensuring that the tissue is the side that will be printed.

5

Allow the ink to dry and remove the tissue from the backing paper.

Collage with tissue prints

These are pages from an altered book with a coastal theme.

The pages were collaged with a variety of neutral coloured papers and handwritten papers.

Prints of photographs on tissue paper were added as the final layers and allow the handwritten text to show through.

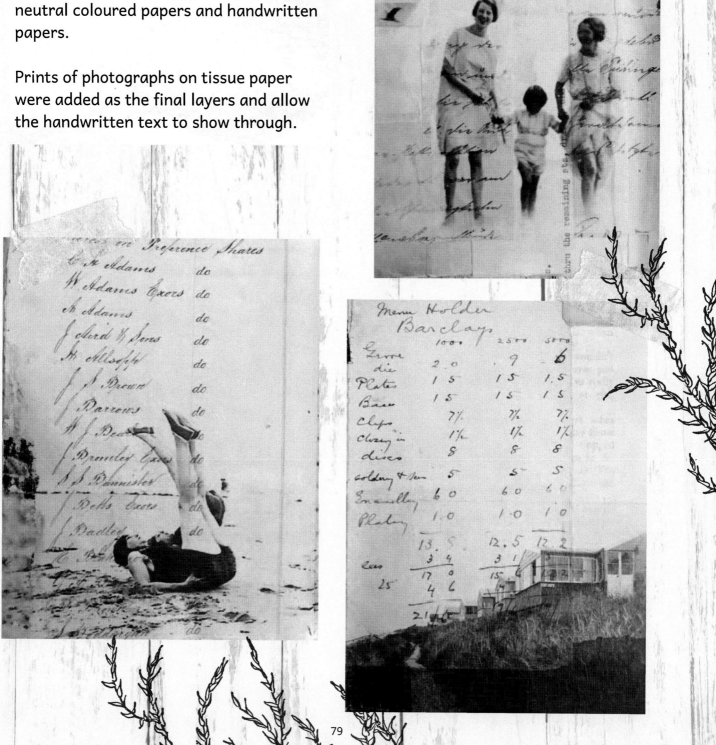

Memory pebbles

Project

You will need:

- **Tissue print of your photograph**
  (see page 78)
- Scissors
- Glue such as Mod Podge
- Fine grit sandpaper – we used P120 grade
- Pebble

This project is one of the easiest in the book, but its simplicity is also part of its beauty. The pairing of seaside images with beach pebbles creates wonderfully nostalgic artworks. Its beauty relies on selecting the right pebble and photograph; enjoy the process of searching for the perfect elements.

Choose a pebble that is smooth, has no marks and is pale in colour. It should be relatively flat rather than domed and oval as opposed to an irregular shape. The size is up to you; ours was about two inches wide.

1

Trim your print to roughly the same shape as your pebble with the edges about 0.5cm smaller than the pebble.

2

Apply a thin coat of Mod Podge to the top surface of your pebble. Gently place your tissue print onto the surface and smooth to remove any creases.

3

Press to ensure that all parts of the print are in contact with the Mod podge.

Leave to dry well.

4

When the tissue has dried, sandpaper the edges of the image so that they blend into the background. Apply a thin coat of Mod Podge to protect the image

Display ideas

Memory pebbles work well displayed in rustic boxes, like these made from cardboard and plaster

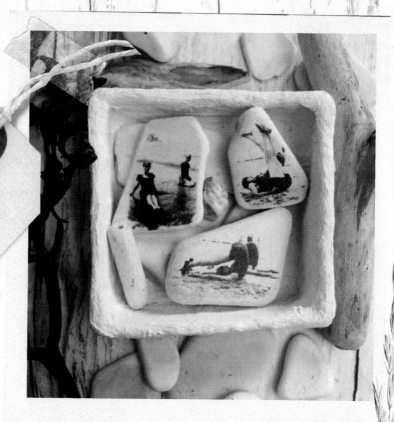

Explore!

Now that you have learned how to print onto tissue paper, you can use the technique to collage onto numerous surfaces. Look out for interesting objects that you could collage with a tissue image such as ceramics, old cutlery, wood, or buttons. The most mundane objects can become very special when a beautiful old photograph is added. We've even collaged onto old bones found on the beach!

Lunaria seed heads

Cut your tissue slightly larger than a dried Lunaria seed head. Very gently apply a thin coat of Mod Podge to the seed head and lightly press the tissue image onto it.

Once dry, trim any excess tissue off with small scissors.

Spoon

Cut your tissue slightly larger than the spoon. Apply a thin coat of Mod Podge to the spoon and lightly press the tissue image onto it, folding the excess around the edge.

Once dry, you may colour with crayons, like in this example.

Poppy seed head

Apply a diluted wash of white gesso to the seed head to make it paler. Cut your tissue into a band to fit around the centre of the seed head, avoiding the very curved areas at the top and bottom to prevent creases in the tissue.

Apply the Mod Podge to the seed head and gently press the tissue image in place.

83

84

Working with

needle and thread

Sacred Magic, Melanie Isis Tinken

"Working with old photographs and the beautifully made everyday objects and papers from the past, leads me to combine them in unexpected ways to invite curiosity and leave room for new invented histories from these exquisite discards."

Wilma Millette

Those Hazy Days of Summer,
Gemma Pepper

Blue Sky,
Anne Misfeldt

Les Deux Frères /
Two Brothers,
Béatrice Beraud

Printing on fabric

You will need:

- Digital scan of a photograph
- Fabric
- Printer
- Freezer paper
- Scissors
- Piece of printer paper to use as a template
- Dye fixative such as Retayne, Bubble Jetset, Rit Dye Fixative

Printing photographs onto fabric opens up a whole world of creative possibilities. You could choose to make a fabric book, a decorative object, or use the print as the substrate for a stitched collage.

There are numerous ways that you can print on fabric including ready made printable sheets, online digital printing services and several ways of using your home computer printer. This is our preferred technique.

The type of fabric that you choose will affect the clarity of the print. A tightly woven fabric (fabric with a high thread count) such as cotton lawn, poplin, organza or fine silk will give a clearer image than a loosely woven fabric such as linen. Think about the effect that you want for your artwork and choose accordingly. All home printers differ in their ability to cope with fabric, but most will only be able to cope with lightweight fabrics.

1

Cut your fabric slightly larger than a piece of printer paper. Treat it with dye fixative according to the instructions (usually soak it, dry and iron).

2

Cut a piece of freezer paper to the same size as the printer paper. Iron it onto your fabric so that the shiny side faces the fabric. Once adhered, trim the fabric to the same size as the freezer paper.

3

Feed the fabric/paper through your printer taking care to make sure the fabric is the side that will be printed.

4

Peel the freezer paper off the fabric. Leave to dry for 30 minutes. Iron the image to set it. (Some dye fixatives are two-part and use a rinse after printing - follow the instructions).

GRANDMOTHER, @ikborduurenjij

Nice Frock, Maria Walker

"Characters can emerge from the landscape of their original story, connecting threads of memory to the present time and contemporary values; creating entirely new histories. Not lost, not forgotten."

Nichola Bendall

The Gathering of Soft Landings, Susie Lafond

Fabric printing tips

If you are making an artwork that will be washed, take extra care and follow the fixative instructions carefully. Some printers have water resistant ink such as Epson Durabright which are less likely to need fixing. Inkjet printers are generally considered to be the best for printing on fabric, but we often use a laser printer which gives good results. Printing on fabric can be a process of trial and error. Experiment with different fabrics and, if possible, different printers. Organza is a great choice for layering as it's almost transparent, so it allows the lower layers to show through whilst heavier fabrics create strong bases for stitched collages

Above - This photograph was printed with an inkjet printer onto unbleached linen with a medium weave. If you prefer a sharper print, use a more tightly woven fabric.

Above - Old letters, certificates, stamps and images were printed onto organza and layered onto a cotton base. They were then embellished with both hand and machine stitch over the top.

Above - A portrait photograph and rose illustrations were printed onto various different shades and weights of linen. Handstitch was added to embellish and hold the pieces in place.

"I am the daughter of a refugee and photographic archives of my father's childhood never existed as they would have been a luxury...I am always amazed when I come across a family archive from the same era that is abandoned and sold in a market. The subject of the photograph Woolly Jumper remains unknown to me and his abandonment unanswered. I have intervened by painting in his jumper using colour after transferring the black and white image onto canvas to emphasise the impermanence of the wearer. We can assume that the boy posed for a private audience. By giving him a public platform, I bear witness and give deserved respect for a life lived."

Edori Fertig

Woolly Jumper, Edori Fertig

60 years, Marjolein van Vessem

My Grandmother's War, Carrie Donohoe

"Old photos have a wonderful sense of depth and character. I feel that working with them honours the individual and also gives them a second lease on life."

Carol Von Stubbe

Bittersweet October, Martina Buiat

Stitching on photographs

Every time we pick up a thread and needle, we are connecting to a strong tradition of stitchers who came before us. Needlework on photographs can increase the value of the memory of the object. Whether you use a sewing machine, hand embroidery, or knitting, you're tapping into the knowledge of your ancestors that has been passed on orally from generation to generation. Make each stitch count.

Embellishing with beads
and sequins

Darning - adding
imagined colours

Extending an image with
machine stitch

Ornate stitching - making
the photograph into a lid

Create Yourself a Colorful Life, Petra Heidrich

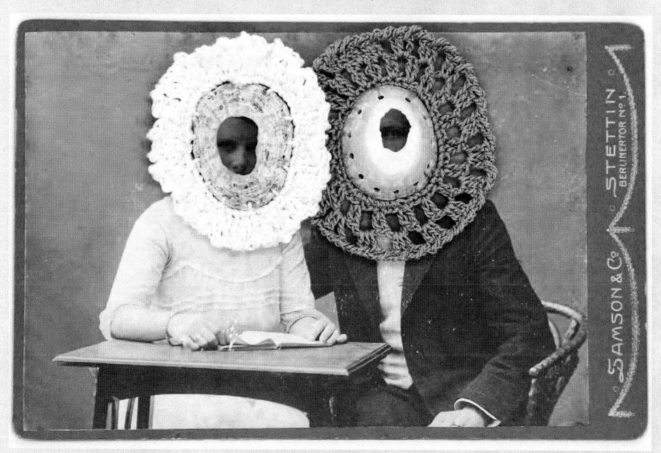

Threadful, Claudia Grabowski

93

Preparing photographs for stitching

Depending on the size of stitches you plan to use, you may need to strengthen the photograph (this technique can be used with other papers too). Small stitches, and in particular those done on a sewing machine, create perforated lines which are likely to cause the photograph to rip.

Our preferred strengthening method is to attach lightweight interfacing to the back of the photograph. Interfacing is a non-woven fabric that's used by dressmakers for stiffening collars and facings. The iron-on type of interfacing is best as you won't need to use glue which would make the photograph more difficult to stitch through.

Cut a piece of interfacing slightly larger than your photograph, and place it with the glue side down on the back of the photograph. Press the back of the photograph for a few seconds with a warm iron until the glue adheres. Trim the excess interfacing off once it's stuck firmly. The photograph is now ready to stitch.

Using a template for cross stitch

Stitching on photographs is easier if you make guide holes for your needle first. Depending on the type of stitch you plan to use, a template may help in lining up the holes.

Use a ruler to draw a grid onto a piece of tracing paper and place it onto your photograph. Make holes through the template and photograph using a thin needle in the places where you will want to stitch. Secure the thread at the back of the photograph with tape and stitch through the pre-made holes.

La Belle aux Joues de Rose, Martina Buiat

Mein Hase, Höchstselbst bs

You, My Little Dandelion, Edina Picco

Der Junge mit der Schultüte, Höchstselbst bs

Beehive quilt

Project

♫ The Temperence Seven -
You're Driving me Crazy

You will need:

- Paper to use as the background for your patchwork; this could be something meaningful like an old letter
- Photograph
- Hexagon - see the template in the next page
- Stiff card such as mount board (matboard)
- Craft knife or scalpel
- Glue stick
- Needle and threads
- Iron-on lightweight interfacing
- Scissors
- Sticky tape

To convert cm to inches see page 148

Tips when choosing your photograph(s)

- decide how many photographs you want to use; we usually use one or two, but you could use more.

- look for contrasts in shade so that you have some light, dark and mid shades to create contrasts in your artwork.

- choose an image that has several areas of interest that can become the focal points of your patches. In ours, there were three people, some buildings, some flowers and interesting features such as the man's flat cap and pipe.

- choose a photograph that's big enough to cut out about 15 - 18 hexagons. The photograph used in this tutorial is 14 x 9cm and the hexagons are 2.5cm wide. If your photograph is larger, use a larger hexagon template. We wouldn't advise going much smaller than 2.5cm hexagons as they will become more difficult to cut out and to stitch.

The saying that 'less is more' is the key to this project. By cutting out small parts of a photograph and rearranging them, you transform it into an intriguing piece of art. The gaps between the patches, and the abstracted parts of the photograph within them cause you to see the different shapes, tones and features within the photograph, rather than just the image.

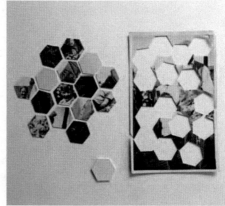

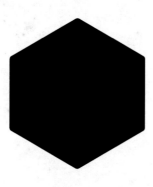

1

Photocopy this template and enlarge or reduce to your required size.

2

Place your template on top of a piece of stiff card and cut the shape out using your scalpel.

3

Identify the parts of your photograph that you want in your patches. They will be more interesting if faces aren't centered in them. In our example we placed the older man's head peeping in from the side of a patch, the lady has a chimney behind her to add interest, and the boy's head is partly cut off at the top. We included the man's button-down cardigan because it was typical of 1930s working class clothing. Include light and dark patches to add contrasts.

The second example is a photograph of some wedding guests. We picked out the key parts of the outfits such as the handbags, shoes and hats. Once you've selected which areas to use, place the template on top and carefully cut around them with the scalpel.

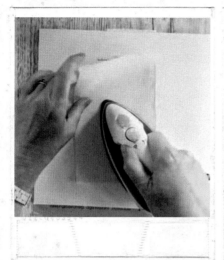

4

Before stitching, the background paper needs to be strengthened by attaching a layer of interfacing to the back. Iron a piece of interfacing to the back of your paper and trim to size so that it's not visible from the front.

5

Lay your patches out in your chosen design, leaving a gap of about 2mm between each patch. Balance out the light, dark and mid shades and decide where you want any patches with key focal points to be placed. When you're happy with the composition, use a small dab of glue to attach them to the background paper.

6

Place your paper onto a soft surface such as a folded towel or a piece of foam and use a needle to make three holes on each side of the patches that are next to another patch.

7

Stitch through the holes using a straight stitch as shown. Secure the end of the thread at the back with a piece of sticky tape. We chose to use a different coloured thread to draw the eye to the patch that we wanted to be the main focal point.

Now that you've learned the technique for making a photograph patchwork, you can explore many different ways of using it.

Try cutting the photograph into different shapes, into strips, using several photographs, adding other papers. Instead of using straight stitches, try others such as cross-stitch

Explore!

Class One (Paradise School), Diane Meyer

Ghosts, from the Series (Her)stories, Flore Gardner

A stitch in time

Project

You will need:

- Paper to use as the base for your piece - we used a blank page from an old book.
- Portrait photograph showing the subject from the waist up.
- Small pieces of decorative paper for the clothing
- Other paper scraps
- Craft knife or scalpel
- Cutting mat
- Glue stick or glue - we used Mod Podge
- Needle and embroidery threads. Choose the finest needle that you are able to manage.
- Tracing paper
- Pencil
- Iron-on lightweight interfacing
- Scissors
- Sticky tape

This is a versatile technique for combining a photograph with collage and stitch. We've used it to enhance the elegance of the portrait but it could be used in a wide range of ways as shown in the following 'Explore' section.

Tips when choosing your papers and threads

- We put a few neutral coloured paper scraps behind the photograph to give the picture a little more texture. This is optional but if you choose to add papers, make sure that they are fairly neutral so that they don't detract from the main image.

- Think about how much you want to change the style of the photograph when you choose paper for the clothing. You could choose aged papers as we have here, which match the age of the photograph. Alternatively, you could choose papers that are a great contrast to the style and totally update the photograph.

- Think about the scale of the pattern on your paper for the clothing. We chose a small floral pattern that matched the scale of the photograph; a larger scale pattern may look less convincing as clothing.

- Decide what colour of thread you want to use. Again, be as conservative or outlandish as you like! We used blue and white for the stitching on the dress and a pale grey for the arm.

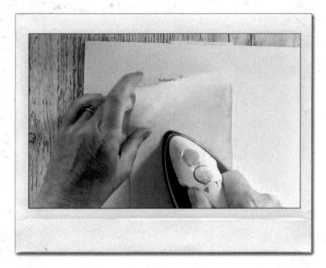

1

Before stitching, strengthen the back of your base paper with interfacing. (See page 94)

2

Place your tracing paper over the photograph. Using a pencil, trace the torso and clothing up to the neckline. Ensure that you trace any features of the clothing and the arms.

In our example, we traced the white fur parts of the dress, the arm, and the folds in the fabric. These will be the lines that you stitch.

3

Using your scalpel, cut out the head and neck of your photograph. Take great care to be as accurate as possible.

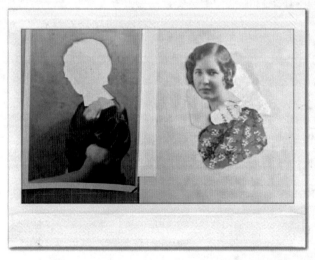

4

Save the remainder of the photograph for future projects (see page 116).

5

Place your photograph onto your base paper along with any other papers that you wish to use. You can put a few small pieces of paper behind the photograph. Roughly tear the paper you wish to use for the clothing into the shape of the body. You can check the position of your pieces by putting your tracing paper over the top to see how it matches up to the traced lines. We like to have the clothing paper smaller than the tracing so that there are parts where the stitching goes onto the backing paper. When you are happy with your composition, put a small amount of glue in the middle of your papers, leaving the edges loose.

6

Place your page onto a soft surface such as a folded towel or piece of foam. Line up your tracing paper so that it accurately meets the neck on your photograph. Use your needle to follow the traced lines and make dotted lines of holes. These will be the holes that you will stitch through.

Thread your needle and attach the loose thread end to the back of your paper with sticky tape.

Stitch through the holes. We used a continuous stitch for the main lines and French Knots for areas where we wanted more height.

Explore different ways to use this technique. Try using different papers for the clothing, or try fabric. Maybe give an old photograph an incongruous makeover with metallics and sequins. Try changing the context of the photograph by adding a pictorial background.

Explore!

Rainbow Explosion, Jamie Rawlings

MY LOVE, MY CHOICE, Marjolein Burbank

Conjoined Yellow, Becky Edmunds

107

Boy with Fish, Helen Chang

Have More Fun, Riikka Fransila

Houston in 3D, Sarah Benesh

Another string to one's bow,
allison anne

Moon Children,
Molly Waite Lund

Working with
scissors

Weaving a dream

Project

You will need:

- 2 Different photos
- Ruler
- Pencil
- Craft knife or scalpel
- Cutting mat
- Glue stick

To convert cm to inches see page 148

This project allows you to combine two or more photographs, to create a new altered image. The outcome is an abstraction that still shows parts of the original images, while also being completely new. It's a metaphor of relationships where individual identities merge to create an even stronger collective synergy, while still remaining visible. You can choose to weave photographs of the same person, maybe taken at different times in their life. You can even explore using three or four different photographs, or alternate documents that once belonged to the individual. You are literally weaving the memory of a person, so don't worry if the portrait is not an accurate likeness of the subject, because it is so much more than just that.

1

Find two photographs that complement each other, or are complete opposites. One in portrait and one in landscape mode work very well together.

2

Take the photograph in portrait mode and turn it over. Measure and cut 0.5cm vertical slits leaving 1cm at the top and 1cm at the bottom uncut.

111

3

Take the photograph in landscape mode and turn it over. Measure 0.5cm horizontal lines across the photograph. Before you cut them, number each strip with a pencil. This will make your life easier when you get to step 5.

4

Cut the horizontal strips all the way.

5

Now you can slide your strips through the portrait photograph, following the patterns on the next page. If the strips become loose, gently push them as close to each other as you can. There may be some strips left at the end.

6

Once you find a winning composition, you can glue it in place. If needed, you can trim off the strip ends.

Following a pattern is one way of playing with this technique, but you don't have to. You can freestyle here, and the results can be just as strong. The combinations really are endless. Why not weave the photo of a singer with a music sheet? Or a wedding photo with a love letter? Good contrasts work just as well – consider weaving two photographs of the same individual as a child and as an older person, or mixing skin colours, or genders. You decide the story you want to tell.

Explore!

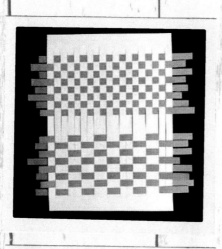
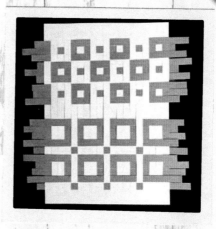

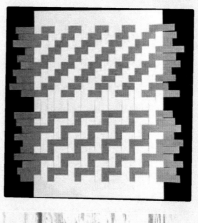
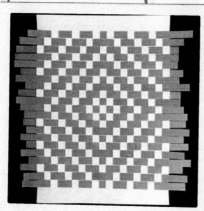
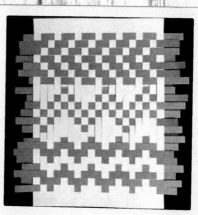

Cousin, Samin Ahmadzadeh

"It's about memory, it's about
losses and it's about who's
left behind."

Ergül Karagözoğlu

"Old photos remind us that we
exist in a grand continuum
with and amongst past,
present & future, and within a
living and conscious timeline."

Helen Chang

Remnants: Betty , Greg Sand

"I've always been drawn to the beauty and melancholy of the found image, the mystery of its story, a moment lost in time. I enjoy breathing life back into that and in doing so becoming part of the same dialogue. It is my way of connecting with and elevating the moment. In a way a kind of time travel, a resurrection of sorts."

Sarah Perkins

Camouflage, Aisla van Dijk

Family History, Sharon Hall Shipp

Negative space

Cutting out the main focal point is a simple and very effective way of altering a photograph. The context of the photograph is immediately changed. It becomes more intriguing and develops a whole new story.

The key to using this technique effectively is to choose a subject with a suitable outline. Once the image is cut out, you will only have the shape left behind to distinguish what was once there. Before cutting out an image, trace it so that you can check how the outline will look.

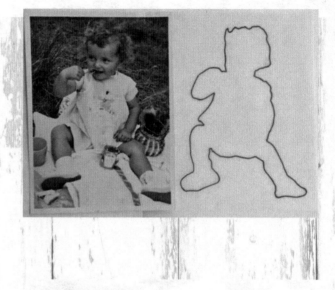

Right - The bent arm and curly hair of this child create a shape that is difficult to recognise.

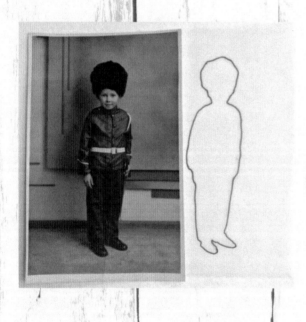

Left - The large hat creates an outline that looks like a disproportionately large head. It is not obvious from the outline that it's a hat.

Right - This photograph has some helpful elements: the high heeled shoe and the stance with the hip thrust forward give clues that it's a mother resting a baby on her hip.

Left - The wide legged stance and the brimmed hat produce an outline that appears masculine.

Having selected an appropriate image, place your photograph onto a cutting mat and use a sharp blade to accurately follow the shape of the figure.

You can now decide whether you want to fill the void with something. In this example we used a piece of a typed letter, but handwritten text, patterned paper or other photographs all work well as a background.

Think about the placement of the background - in this example we ensured that the word 'love' was placed where the boy's heart would be.

"Thoughtful use of negative space can be very powerful within your art.

This piece entitled 'Refugee', is about my mother's experience as a refugee leaving Lithuania in 1940.

I cut out the photograph of a child with a suitcase and used the empty space to represent the abandoned home. The fir trees in the background represent the forest where she played as a child, and the text in the negative space is from a book about the town where she lived. The roses represent the beautiful garden that her parents eventually had when they were able to rebuild their lives after the war." JC

Gone to Summer, Kelly Hayes

I'm Not Your Flower, Kelley Clink

118

The Future is Each Other, Lisbeth Sogard-Hoyer

Double Daydream, Stephen Sheffield

Family Tree, Lisa Drake

119

Path to the City, Marion Quinn

Alone and Together

1-hour project

♫ Yann Tiersen - Le Matin

You will need:

- 2 Photographs
- 2 Used tea bags, dry
- Small scissors
- Book pages
- Craft knife or scalpel
- Tweezers
- Cutting mat
- PVA glue

1

Take a tea bag and using a pair of small scissors cut a horizontal slit in the back.

2

Remove the tea through the slit. Repeat with the second tea bag.

3

Pick two photographs and cut out the silhouettes.

4

Brush the front of the cutouts with PVA glue.

5

Using tweezers, gently slide the photographs through the slit on the tea bags.

6

Cut words out from an old book.

7

Collage the words onto the tag to caption your photographs.

Contemplation,
Marcia Conlon

The Flowers Outside Mum's House,
Carly Guppy

Rosalie,
Michael Tietz-Geldenhuys

Celebrate Life,
Anja Brunt

Stock photographs

1-hour project

You will need:

- Photograph
- Paper
- Tracing paper
- Pen
- Ruler
- Scissors
- Craft knife or scalpel
- Glue stick

This is a fun, quick project on making cubes by using a template and folding photographs. Group photographs work well as there are lots of faces to be seen as you turn the cubes over.

In this example we made the cubes 15mm, the same size as Oxo cubes (bouillon cubes) so that they would fit into this old tin. These look great displayed in the tin, and make the photograph even more enticing to study.

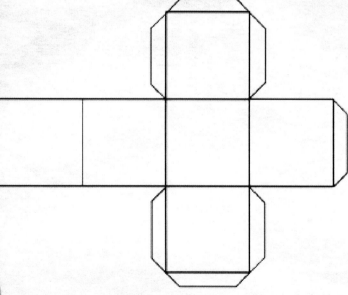

1

Choose your photograph and then make a cube template which covers the main parts of your photograph (see step 2 overleaf).

To make your cube template draw one like the one above or scan this one and size accordingly.

2

Copy the template on to tracing paper and place on top of your photograph. Identify which parts of the image you want on the cube.

3

Tape the template to the edge of the photograph and carefully cut out around the edges of the template.

4

Fold along all of the lines shown on the template

5

Use a glue stick to apply glue to the tabs. Fold into a cube shape with the glued tabs on the inside.

Hilo Rojo (Red Thread), Adriana Pardo

"I create a portal to the past with an assemblage of souls from another time."

Bobbie Holmes

Stopover, Veronika Lambertucci

Window Dresser, Madcollage

Amsterdam, Dorothée Mesander

Working with

nature

Using natural materials

Old photographs and natural materials are a perfect coupling. The faded and fragile beauty of dried leaves and flowers acts as a metaphor for the passage of time, and for the time that has passed since our photographs were taken. At their most simplistic, natural elements are beautiful and they add texture and interest, but they can also add a new layer of memories to a piece of art; memories of where they were found, who you were with, or what you were feeling at the time they came into your possession.

Natural elements can be used as a surface on which to collage, as a frame, as an embellishment, or as a base structure. Look out for interesting pieces. Let your imagination run free as you consider how to combine them with a photograph.

This sea-worn limpet shell made a perfect frame for a tiny beach photograph, but any vaguely round object could be used in a similar way. Strengthen the photograph as shown on page 94, before stitching through and around the shell to suspend the photograph in the middle.

This photograph from 1897 was very damaged. Stitch was used to accentuate the disintegrated edges and the sepia coloured dried petals look as though they are relics from the garden.

Roommates Ficus, Puur Anders

SAUDADE "Love remains", Claudia Freundt Delta

Family Portrait, Ihosvany Plasencia

Forget Me Not, Ergül Karagözoğlu

Wallflower, Frances Willoughby

Daphne Girl, Erika Lujano

Lost and Found, Frances Willoughby

Anonymous, Tolga Akmermer

Mother, Daniela Merino

Woodland dress

Project

You will need:

- Carte de Visite (CDV) featuring a dress
- Dried flowers or moss
- Wooden box
- Cardboard tube
- Twine
- Pruning shears or scissors
- Pencil
- PVA glue

This tutorial shows you how to use flowers and other natural elements to transform a photograph into a three dimensional sculpture. The invitation here is to go big and to create unrealistic silhouettes inflating the skirt disproportionately.

1

Look for a CDV that only shows a part of the dress, ideally cropped just under the waist. Select dried flowers that match the tone, colour, or atmosphere of the photo.

2

Pick the nicest looking flowers from the bunch and keep to the side. These will be used to decorate the skirt.

3

Mark the depth of the wooden box
on the carboard tube.

4

Cut 2cm inside of the line marked.

5

Glue the cardboard tube to the
back of the CDV, in the top section.
Let dry.

6

Place the CDV inside the box and
start cutting the stems long enough
to fit tucked under the photograph.

7

Once you have enough flowers to create the bulk of the skirt, tie in place with a piece of twine.

8

Glue the bouquet in the bottom part of the box. Place the CDV on top, hiding the twine knot. You want the flowers to be as aligned as possible with the dress.

9

Pick one of the nicer flowers that you kept aside. Following the lines of the dress and starting at the waist, glue the flowers onto the CDV one at a time.

10

Once you have completed covering the dress with flowers, fill in any gaps with petals or leaves.

Explore!

The beauty of this tutorial is that you can use what you have available locally. Instead of flowers why not use dried moss or leaves?

Or if you live near the sea, try seaweed and shells.

The best boxes are rectangular, so that you have plenty of room for an exagerated and dramatic skirt. The box used in the tutorial is a vintage brick mould, but you can use a wine box instead, which can be painted or decoupaged like in the example above.

Untitled, Mr What & Mrs Why

Sheila, Katie McCraw

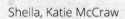

Untitled, Eve Baldry

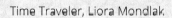

Time Traveler, Liora Mondlak.

Printables

Finding old photographs to use in your artwork is great fun. However, if you need some images to get you started, we've included some of our found photographs and ephemera here. Scan and resize as you wish, or go to www.artfulmemoriesbook.com to download.

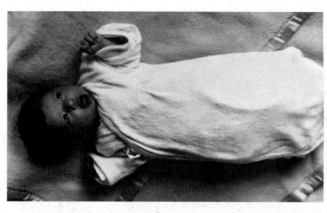

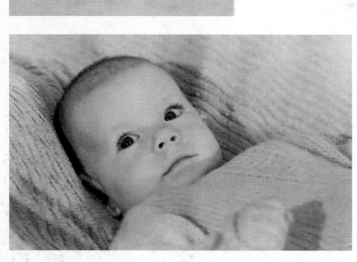
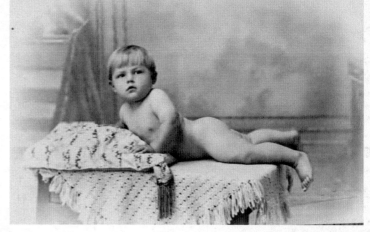

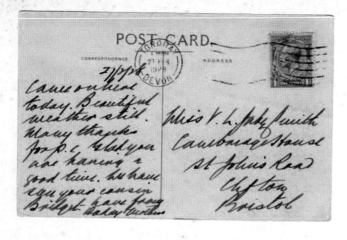

POST CARD

CORRESPONDENCE — ADDRESS

Came out here
today. Beautiful
weather still.
Many thanks
for p.c. Glad you
was having a
good time. We have
seen your cousin
Billy & have from
today Mother

Miss V. L. [?] Smith
Cambridge House
St John's Road
Clifton
Bristol

COMPAGNIE DU SOLEIL
Société anonyme d'Assurances à Primes fixes contre l'Incendie
FONDÉE EN 1829
CAPITAL SOCIAL : 6.000.000
Siège à Paris, Rue de Châteaudun, N° 44

Madame René Pelletier

à Saint-Dizier

(Haute-Marne)

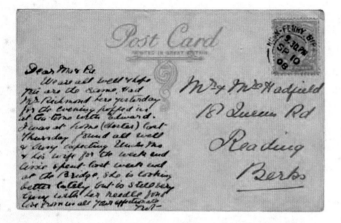

Post Card
PRINTED IN GREAT BRITAIN

Dear Mr & Ro
We are all well & hope
you are the same. Had
Mr Richmond here yesterday
for the evening popped in
at tea time with Edward.
I was at home (Hartes) last
Thursday found all well
& very capering. Uncle Jno
& his wife for the week end
Annie spent last week end
at the Bridge, she is looking
better lately but is still very
funny with her needle and
love from us all Your affectionate
Nell —

Mr & Mrs Hadfield
18 Queens Rd
Reading
Berks

Miss Chalk
128 Argyle Road
West Ealing
W.

Tools and materials

We use a wide range of tools and materials in this book and, like most artists, we have our favourite brands. We will tell you about the materials that we like but many of them can be substituted so, before buying any new supplies, see if you already have materials that could be used.

Glues

Foam pads - double sided pads that provide instant adhesion. Suitable when you want a 3D effect as the pad will make the item you are sticking stand proud of the background.

Glue sticks - sometimes the easier option is the most overlooked. A good old fashioned glue stick can go a long way, and it's quicker to dry than most liquid glues. We recommend Pritt and Office Depot.

Hot glue - sold in solid sticks which are fed through a glue gun that melts the glue. Useful for awkward gaps and sticking porous and non-porous materials.

Mod Podge - (short for 'modern decoupage' if you were wondering!) used as a glue, sealant and for image transfers. It is slightly thinner than PVA glue and enables thin materials, such as tissue paper, to be adhered without any lumps. Available in various versions including matte and gloss; we use the matte version. In our experience it doesn't yellow with age.

PVA - a useful general glue. Slightly thicker than Mod Podge so can adhere heavier papers. Not archival so may yellow with age

Spray mount - repositionable spray mount can be used for attaching thin papers such as tissue to a carrier sheet so that it can be fed through a printer, and then peeled off.

Cutting equipment

Craft knife or scalpel - very sharp fine blade which allows for precise cutting. Packs of spare blades can be bought.

Cutting mat - 'self-sealing' mats maintain a smooth surface because the marks made with a blade close up instantly.

Scissors - of various sizes. Large general purpose scissors for non-detailed work, small fine-pointed scissors for intricate work. Look after your scissors and use a sharpener to keep them in good condition.

Pens and paints

Acrylic paint - heavy body or fluid; either are fine for painting onto photographs. The more expensive brands, such as Liquitex and Golden, have a higher amount of pigment but aren't essential for the projects in this book.

Felt tips / marker pens - using what you already have is absolutely ok. For precision work we recommend Point 88 fineliners by Stabilo. The metal tip can be used against a ruler without smudging, so you can colour all along the white frame of a photograph. There are 55 vibrant colours from which to choose.

Gesso - available in white, black and clear. Gesso is a primer; applying it to any surface enables you to then add other materials such as paint and ink.

Neocolour II crayons - made by Caran D'ache, these are water soluble wax pastels. They produce beautiful creamy colours and mix well with acrylic paints and gesso.

Pencils - for precise work, use a mechanical pencil (0.5mm) so that you always have a fine point.

Posca pens - water based paint markers that work on all surfaces. They produce an opaque, chalky looking finish.

Papers

Acetate sheets - transparent sheets. Available clear or coloured, they are very versatile. Make sure you choose the printable and acid free version.

Ephemera / found papers - terms generally used for old handwritten letters, documents, book pages, postcards; the sort of things you might expect to find in an old bureau. Found papers combine well with old photographs. Look for them in charity shops, flea markets and auctions. Etsy and Ebay are a great source with sellers selling 'ephemera packs' of mixed papers. If you cannot find originals, look for digital downloads of vintage papers online. If you use old paper when you print a digital download, you can get an authentically old looking document.

Freezer paper - a paper product that has a plastic coating on one side. The plastic side can be ironed onto fabric to act as a carrier sheet so that fabric can be fed through a printer. Readily available in the USA and online elsewhere (often sold with quilting supplies).

Photographs - the majority of our work is made using sepia or black and white, but old colour photographs can work well too. See page 13 for details on sourcing old photographs.

Tissue paper - for creating tissue prints find the most transparent available. Some tissue paper has a very white, fibrous look, and should be avoided. The ideal tissue is very thin and becomes almost transparent when glued with Mod Podge. If you want your project to be archival we suggest using acid-free tissue, which won't discolour over time.

Tracing paper - useful for testing out compositions. Ours is 100gm but any will suffice.

Needlework and fabrics

Beads - these are a matter of preference. You may want to use various sizes, colours or materials. In 'Sleeping In A Matchbox' we used 2mm glass beads, which require particularly thin needles. English beading needles have a smaller eye, so the needle remains the same width all the way along, making them ideal for very small beadwork.

Dye fixative - a solution that is used to treat fabric so that it can be printed with an inkjet printer. Popular brands are Retayne, Bubble Jetset, and Rit Dye Fixative. Fabric can be printed without using a fixative, but it may fade or lose its clarity.

Interfacing - a non-woven fabric used by dressmakers for stiffening. It is available in various weights; we use lightweight for strengthening papers and photographs prior to stitching them. It has dried glue on one side which is activated by ironing with a hot iron.

Needles - for stitching through a photograph the needle needs to be able to pierce the paper easily, but not create too large a hole. This will be trial and error depending on how thick your photograph paper is. Choose the thread you wish to use and then use the finest needle that is able to pierce the paper. For beading (Sleeping in a Matchbox) the needle needs to be fine enough to thread through your beads.

Threads - dressmaking thread, embroidery floss, silk threads, or linen can all be used. Decide on what appearance you want; embroidery thread or silk will give a delicate finish whilst dressmaking thread or linen may look more utilitarian. The subject matter of your photographs may help decide which will work better. In 'A Stitch In Time' we matched the floral papers with embroidery threads, whereas 'Beehive Quilt' worked better with household thread.

General

Glue brushes - we use a wide, fairly firm brush for applying glue. Make sure you put the brush in water straight after use.

Microglaze - an acid free sealer with a similar texture to Vaseline, made by Judikins (available online).

Paint brushes - a selection of brushes in different sizes will enable you to cover large areas as well as small details.

Ruler - we have provided all measurements in metric.

> To convert:
> centimetres to inches, multiply by 0.4
> milimetres to inches, multiply by 0.04

When using a ruler as a guide for cutting, use one with a metal edge to prevent you slicing the edge.

Sandpaper - we use a fine grit (P120) sandpaper for making sharp edges on paper disappear and for distressing surfaces.

Containers

Look out for interesting small boxes and tins. Once you start looking you will spot them everywhere; stationery containers, haberdashery, sardine tins, first aid supplies, lozenge tins. Old matchboxes can be beautiful. If you can't find a vintage one there are often old matchbox labels for sale on eBay that you could stick onto a new matchbox.

Natural elements

Having a stash of natural elements to hand can be inspirational when making artworks. Our staples are dried flowers, seed heads, pebbles, shells, driftwood, pressed leaves/flowers and lichen.

Wealth Assets Manager,
Carol Von Stubbe

The Family Pawtraits,
Melanie Barnes

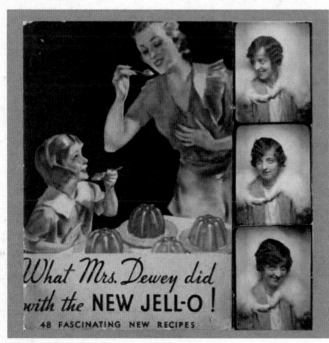

Double Entendre,
Barbara Buckles

Stringing Along,
Marsha Balian

Contributors

Adriana Pardo
Agnieszka Zając
Ailsa Mitchell
Aisla van Dijk
allison anne
Andrea Baudo Queyroulet
Anja Brunt
Anke Teuscher
Anna Müller
Anna van der Putte
Anne Misfeldt
Barbara Buckles
Becky Edmunds
Beverly Silva
Bobbie Holmes
Béatrice Beraud
Carly Guppy
Carol Von Stubbe
Carrie Donohoe
Carrie Mason
Cindy Kuijpers
Claire Steele
Claudia Freundt Delta
Claudia Grabowski
Cláudia Brandão
Colleen Monette
Damla Sandal
Daniela Merino
Debbie Keller
Deborah Saul
Denise ((bonaimo)) Sarram
Diane Meyer
Dorothee Mesander
Edina Picco
Edori Fertig
Elizabeth Burman
Ellen Haines
Emily Glink

Ergül Karagözoğlu
Erika Lujano
Eve Baldry
Eve Lumai Bridges
Flore Gardner
Frances Willoughby
Francesca Artoni
Francesca Lawrence
Gedimina Statuleviciene (Photodido)
Gemma Pepper
Greg Sand
Helen Chang
Höchstselbst bs
Ian Tothill
Ihosvany Plasencia
@ikborduurenjij
Jade Gilbert
Jamie Rawlings
Janet Reid
Jennifer Black
Jo Hudson
Kamryn Shawron
Karla Fuller
Katie McCraw
Katrin Ruhnau
Kelley Clink
Kelly Bymers
Kelly Hayes
Lana Turner
Larysa Hnativ
Linda Sandoval
Liora Mondlak
Lisa Drake
Lisa Goddard
Lisbeth Sogard-Hoyer
Lola Marín
Lucía D'Elía Lago
Madcollage

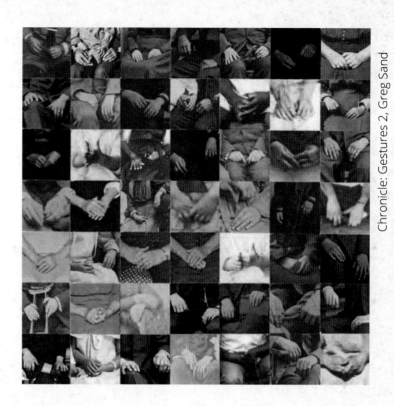

Chronicle: Gestures 2, Greg Sand

Maggie Horvath
Mano Kellner
Marcia Conlon
Margarete Miller
Maria Walker
Marion Quinn
Marjolein Burbank
Marjolein van Vessem
Marsha Balian
Martina Buiat
Mauricio Mo
Melanie Barnes
Melanie Isis Tinken
Michael Tietz-Geldenhuys
Molly Waite Lund
Mr What & Mrs Why
Muriel Binet
Naomi Vona
Natasha Pastrana
Nichola Bendall
Nicole Watson
Ottavia Marchiori
Pat Laffin
Petra Heidrich
Photodido
Pim van Huisseling

Puur Anders
Ramona Samuels
Rene' Alink
Riikka Fransila
Sabine Remy
Samin Ahmadzadeh
Sandra Vydmonte (Photodido)
Sarah Benesh
Sarah Perkins
Sharon Hall Shipp
Silke Kreuznacht
Silvia Pérez Sanz
Sofia Shearring
Sonya Carnes
Stephen Sheffield
Steven Jans
Studio Four Corners
Susie Lafond
Tolga Akmermer
Twiggy Boyer
Valentina Cozzi
Veronika Lambertucci
Victoria Gray
Wilma Millette
Xoana Elias
Zoë Heath

Index

Acknowledgements

"Let us be grateful to the people who make us happy; they are the charming gardeners who make our souls blossom."

Marcel Proust

But for a Mother's Love, Ellen Haines

We would like to extend our thanks to:

- the beautiful, supportive and inspiring community of Instagram artists, for being a thriving and positive force in our lives;
- all the artists who entered artworks to be considered for the book, your response went so far beyond our expectations and we can't thank you enough for making Beauty;
- all the artists who shared their precious words on the use of photographs, thank you for articulating your love with such depth;
- Kit Davey for the book structure that was adapted to create "All Dressed Up";
- our trusted friends, Fiona Cumming, Jen Worden and Peter Brooks for proofreading the book and offering your generous advice;
- Andrew Smith for proofreading and all the technical support;
- The Graphics Fairy.com for some prints used within the projects;
- Photo Trouvée Magazine, for creating such a warm and intimate space for us lovers of the found image.

Jack would like to express his utmost gratitude to:

- Julia Cameron (The Artist's Way) and Sarah Maker (Are You Book Enough?) for reigniting a spark;
- Martha and Neruma, for the encouraging words during the process of writing the book, you're my rays of sunshine during self-doubt rains;
- Agnese, for your continuous gentle presence;
- my Nonna, who inspired some of the thoughts on closure and healing during grief;
- Craig, for always encouraging change and growth, for your unconditional support, and for all the home cooked lunches during busy book days;
- my co-author Jane, for having asked me to write the book with you in the first place, I feel humbled and privileged to be sailing on this tall ship with you.

Jane would like to express her thanks to:

- Dylan, Maddy, Seb and Conor, for your endless acceptance and encouragement of my odd ways;
- My Mum, an artist and stoic, for her constant warmth, kindness and gentleness and my Dad, for all that I learned from sitting at his jewellery bench watching him create;
- My brothers, Bill, Pete and Mark for the self-confidence that is borne out of a solid family;
- Sian Martin for teaching me so much and encouraging me to avoid the obvious;
- Chris Dart for your boundless enthusiasm and encouragement... you unknowingly started me off on this path;
- My network of friends, old and new and particularly Jane and Lisa, my frequent partners in crime;
- Jack, for agreeing to join me on this gentle adventure; you have made every moment of it a joy.

About the authors

Jane Chipp is a collage, assemblage and textile artist based in Somerset, UK.

She celebrates the lives of forgotten people by making artworks using found objects, old papers and photographs. She aims to engender a connection to the past and a recognition of the basic similarities between us and our predecessors, that the human experience is based on the same emotions, fears and pleasures regardless of the century.

Jane is a tutor and Design Team member for The Graphics Fairy.com. Her work has featured in several publications including 'Collage Care' by Laurie Kanyer, Somerset Studio magazine by Stampington publications and Photo Trouvee Magazine and book.

Jane's work is privately owned in the UK, USA, Hong Kong, Australia, Germany, Korea and Denmark and a piece is held in the Kanyer Collection.

www.janechipp.art

Jack Ravi is a self-taught artist, living and working in the UK.

He makes collage and assemblage art with found objects. His work aims to evoke memory, to draw visual poems that turn anonymity into identity. He works with curiosity and with a sense of wonder, with references that come from the collective unconscious, exploring themes like loss and play, memory and identity, masculinity and gender norms.

His work was featured in the book #BlackCollagesMatter, by Brittany M. Reid (Paper Heart Gallery) and in the Photo Trouvee Magazine Book by Juliana Naufel and Twiggy Boyer.

Jack's work is privately owned in the UK, USA, Italy, Canada, Germany, The Netherlands and Australia.

www.jackravi.com

Thank you for reading our book, we hope it has inspired you to make some art.

We'd love it if you would help us to spread the word by **leaving a review on Amazon.**

With love, Jack and Jane